Yacker™ Stickers make your words Sing

My heart 2 heart™

Keyhole

Diary

Writing is the Key to the whole thing

my lock key day

lookee lookee

luckee luckee

oh, cool! Stickers

Linda Campbell Franklin, ARTIST
Ninda Dumont, EDITOR

FINE print
PUBLISHING

Fine Print Publishing Company
Longwood, Florida

My Heart 2 Heart Diary: Keyhole

Fine Print Publishing Company
P.O. Box 916401
Longwood, Florida 32791-6401

ISBN 978-0-9640713-0-8

This book is printed on acid-free paper.

Created in the U.S.A. & Printed in China

31 33 34 32

www.fprint.net

Hello!

Here are 128 pages just for you to make into your very own book.

Draw my face!

Most pages are lined and have four paragraphs. This is a book where you can write, draw, and color. Draw your own t-shirts, coins, signs, flowers, faces!

When you see a "word balloon" coming from an animal's mouth you can fill it in with what the animal might say, or use word-pictures.

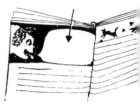

When you see a blank full-page or half-page with little corner decorations you can paste in a photo or draw something.

The paper in this book is pretty thick, but be careful: dark felt-tip pen markers show through on the other side. Color pencils work best and you can "mix" colors right on the page. (More about this on the page to your left.)

Decorate with color dots, gold stars . . . even banana stickers (there are two pages for fruit stickers). Or use fancy stickers or rubber stamps. Create your very own book—to write in, draw in, paste in, and keep for a whole year.

Have fun!

Ninda Dumont

When one door closes
another opens.

Lost time is never found.

Bad excuses are
worse than none.

What goes around comes around.

ork begun is work half done.

WORK

Happiness is meant to be shared.

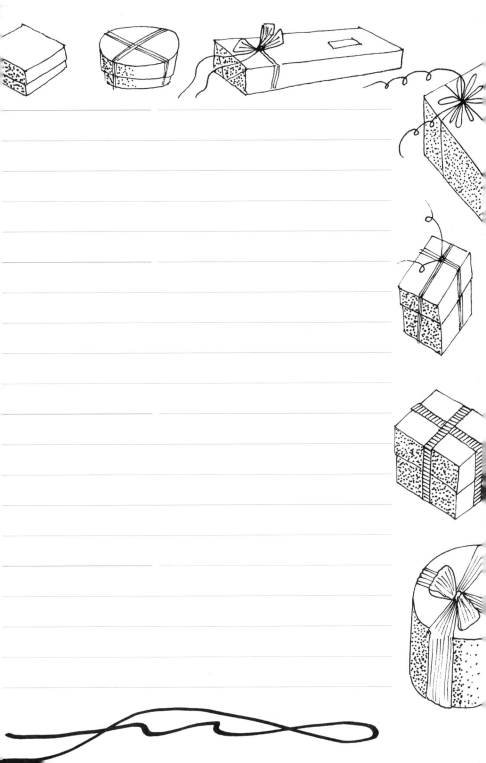

Turn over a
new leaf.

Courtesy costs nothing.

Many littles

make a lot.

put off 'til tomorrow

Never

what you can do today.

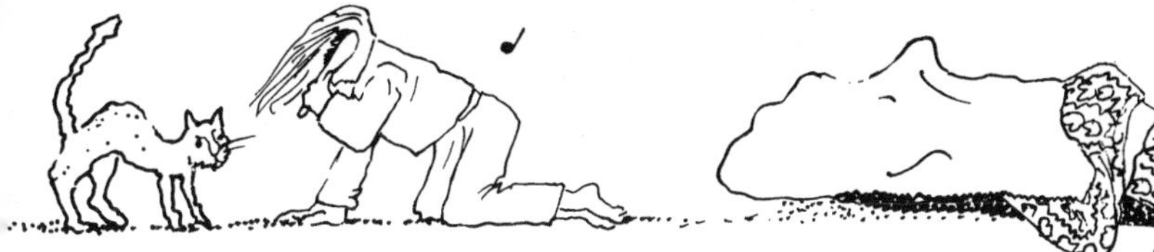

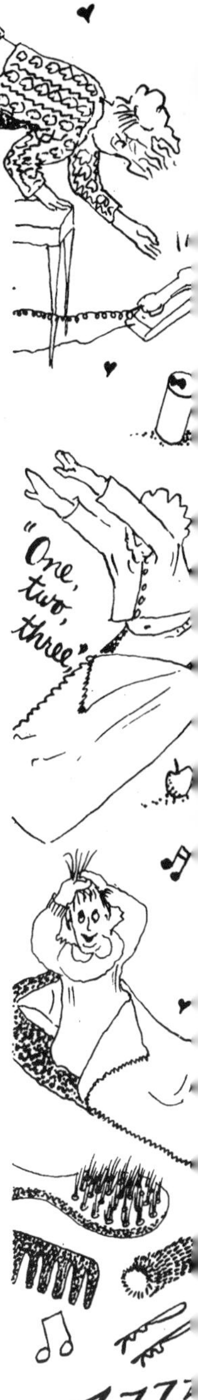
"One, two, three"

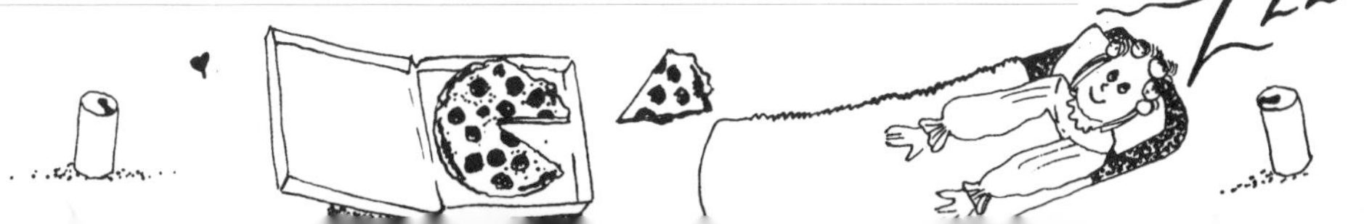
ZZZ

A stitch in time saves nin-

If you let your mind

play part of the time

it will work better **all of the time !**

Out of sight ...

... *out of mind.*

Print your own fingerprints by pressing finger on inked stamp pad, then on page. Blot them with a sheet of paper towel overnight to keep them from getting smeared.

Don't
forget
me!

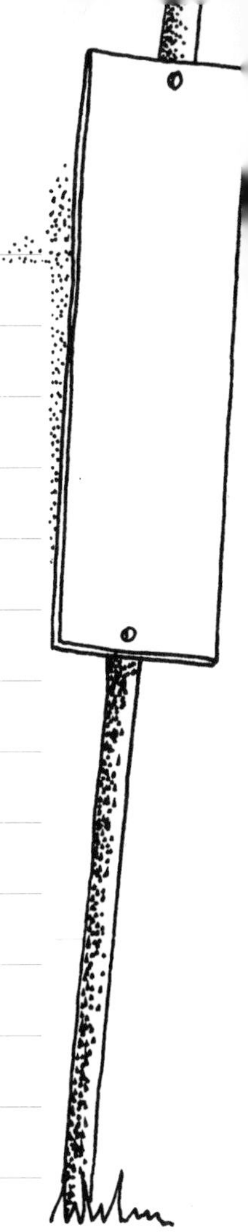

NO
WHINING
PAST THIS
POINT

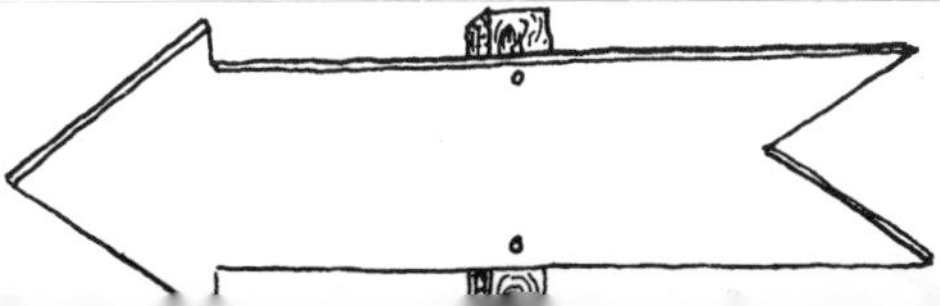

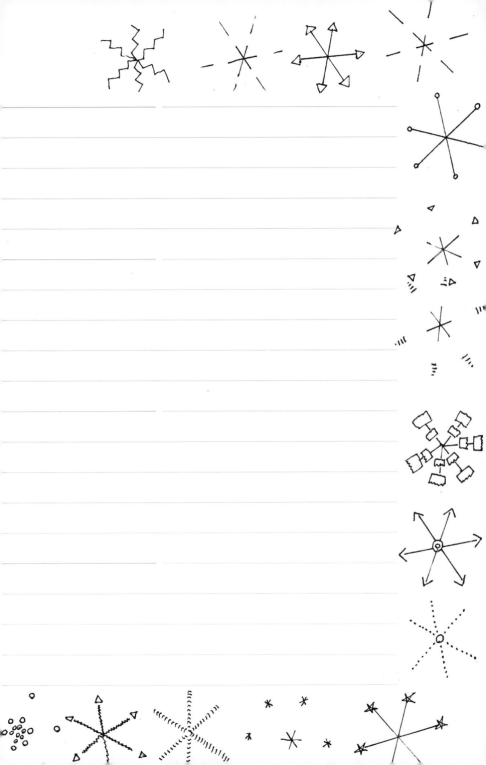

You only have one chance

to make a first impression.

A willing min

makes a light foot.

Be kind to al

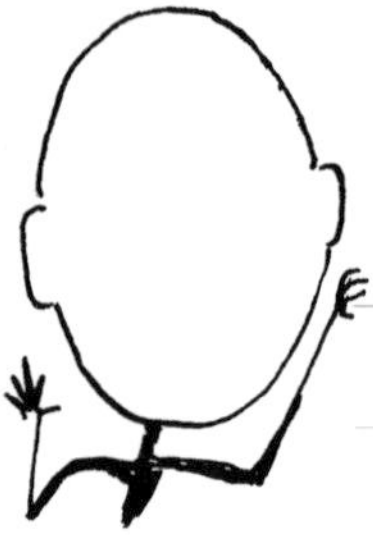
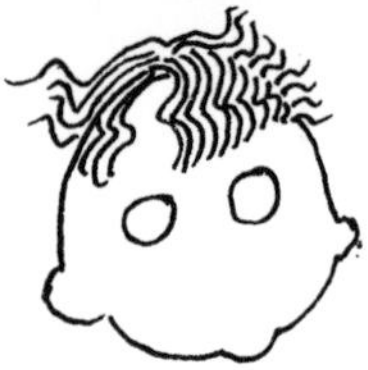
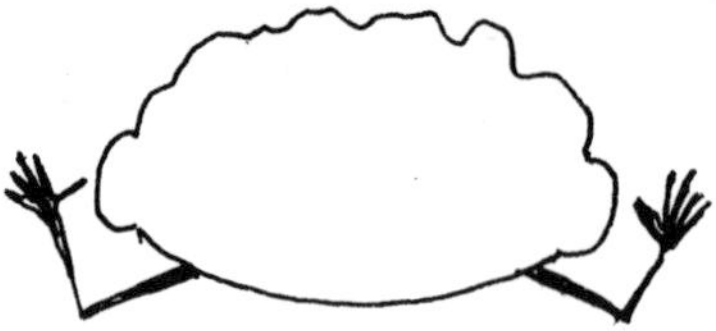
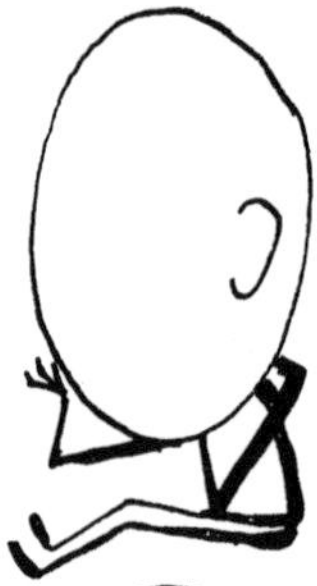
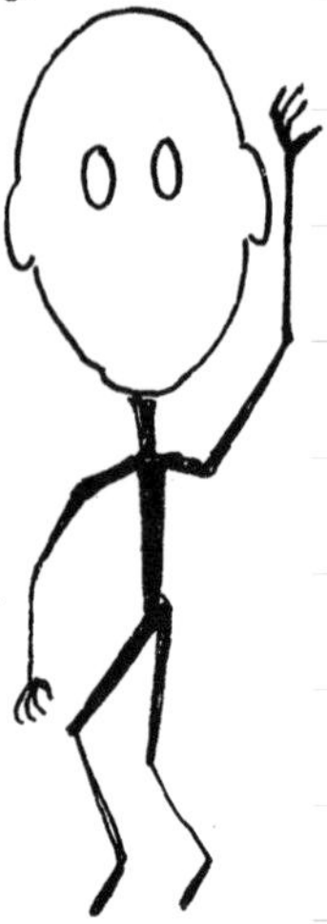
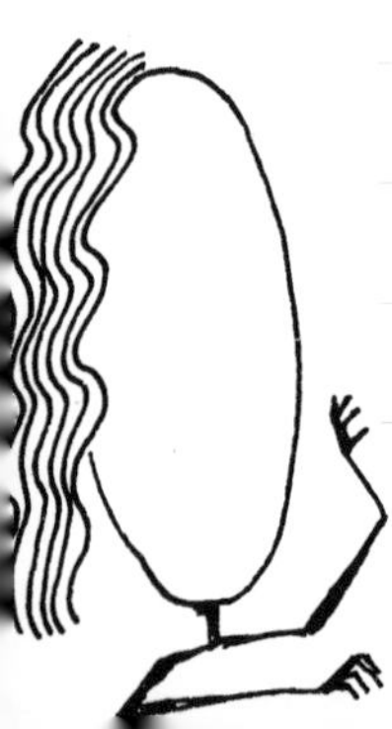
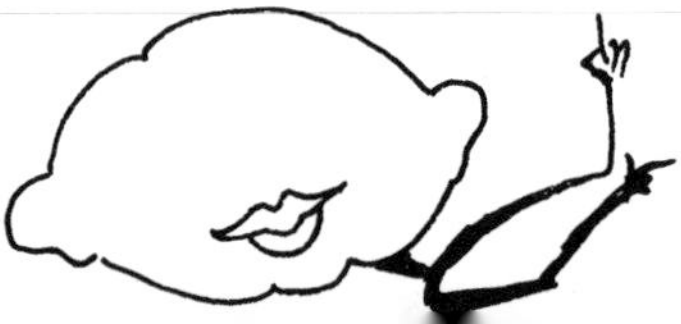
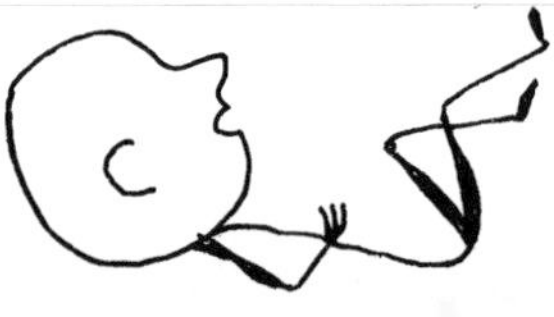

"After you!"

"You're welcome."

Beauty is as beauty does.

"I'll be glad to do it."

"Let me help"

"I apologize"

"Let's be friends."

"Don't cry, it's okay."

Those who give their be

xpect it in return.

Absence makes the

heart grow fonder.

Honesty is its own reward.

ifferent strokes for

different folks.

Look before you leap! *

THE LAST WORD

HAVE FUN

Vacation

Birthdays

September 9   17

1   26   18   August   10   Happy   March   19   2

27   December   July   11   Slurp   February   12   3

Holidays

Christmas

Hanukka

Kwanzaa

4th of July

Memorial Day

Best

Actors

Advice

Afterschool events

Attitude

Bands & music

Behaved person

Boys

Breakfast

Bumper sticker

Chore/job

Classes

Colors

Foods

Friends

Hobbies

Magazines

"WORST

Actors

Advice

Afterschool events

Attitude

Bands & music

Behaved person

Boys

Breakfast

Bumper sticker

Chore/job

Classes

Colors

Foods

Friends

Hobbies

Magazines

Best

Motto
Movies
Phone friend
Sweet treat
Teachers
Time to dream
Time to think
Time to write
Toys
T-shirt slogans
TV shows
Videos
Way to start day
Way to end day
Words
Writer

Worst

Motto
Movies
Phone friend
Sweet treat
Teachers
Time to dream
Time to think
Time to write
Toys
T-shirt slogans
TV shows
Videos
Way to start day
Way to end day
Words
Writer

What I Read, Saw, Heard and Felt

more of
What I Read, Saw, Heard and Felt

Picture Album

Resolutions
for next year